ANIMAL HOMES

**McGraw-Hill
Children's Publishing**

A Division of The McGraw-Hill Companies

This edition published in the United States in 2002 by
Peter Bedrick Books, an imprint of
McGraw-Hill Children's Publishing,
A Division of The McGraw-Hill Companies
8787 Orion Place
Columbus, OH 43240

www.MHkids.com

ISBN 0-87226-695-8

Library of Congress Cataloging-in-Publication Data is on file with the publisher.

Animal Homes created and produced by

McRae Books

via de' Rustici, 5, Florence (Italy)
tel. +39 055 264 384
fax +39 055 212 573
e-mail: mcrae@tin.it

Project Manager: Anne McRae
Graphic Design: Marco Nardi
Illustrations: Sabrina Marconi, Fiammetta Dogi, Paola Holguín, Antonella Pastorelli
Picture Research: Holly Willis
Editing: Cath Senker
Layout and cutouts: Adriano Nardi, Laura Ottina, Filippo Delle Monache

Color separations: Litocolor (Florence)
Printed and bound by Artegrafica, Verona (Italy)

DESERTS

Text by Christina Longman
Illustrations by Sabrina Marconi

PETER BEDRICK BOOKS

Table of Contents

Introduction

Over a fifth of our world is desert. In deserts, very little rain falls. Water is vital for life, so few plants are able to grow in deserts. Food for animals is scarce. But both plants and animals have found clever ways of surviving in the harsh environment. Most of the world's deserts are near the equator, an imaginary line running around the earth. These areas are hot, with temperatures reaching 130°F (54°C). Yet deserts can be freezing cold at night.

Desert scenes

When we think of deserts, we imagine endless stretches of sand under a burning sun. Yet sand covers only a small part of hot deserts. Large areas are covered in gravel and boulders. The idea of deserts being hot, sandy, and empty has inspired famous books, movies, and other works of art. But as we shall see, deserts are far from empty. They hide many fascinating secrets.

This map shows deserts and the areas that are becoming deserts in the world today.

Rare rain

Deserts occur in areas that receive less than 10 inches (250 mm) of rain a year. A typical desert, such as in Egypt, gets only 2 inches (50 mm) of rain a month in the wet season.

Desert tracks

Snakes and other reptiles are common in deserts. Their scaly skin helps to keep them moist. It also prevents them from dehydrating, or losing too much water. Desert reptiles get the water they need from the meat they eat. Their urine has so little water in it that it is almost solid. This helps the animal to save water. Desert snakes speed across the sand in a sidewinding manner, so they touch the hot ground as little as possible. A striped trail is left behind on the sand.

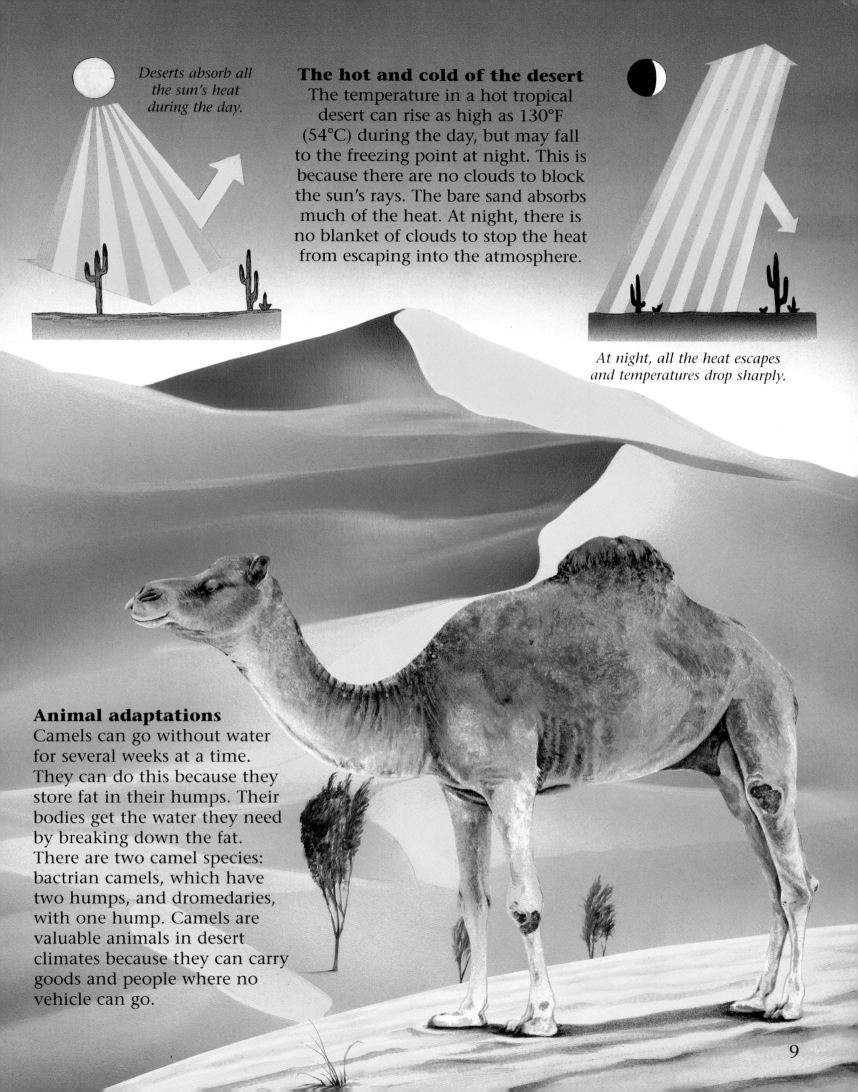

Deserts absorb all the sun's heat during the day.

The hot and cold of the desert

The temperature in a hot tropical desert can rise as high as 130°F (54°C) during the day, but may fall to the freezing point at night. This is because there are no clouds to block the sun's rays. The bare sand absorbs much of the heat. At night, there is no blanket of clouds to stop the heat from escaping into the atmosphere.

At night, all the heat escapes and temperatures drop sharply.

Animal adaptations

Camels can go without water for several weeks at a time. They can do this because they store fat in their humps. Their bodies get the water they need by breaking down the fat. There are two camel species: bactrian camels, which have two humps, and dromedaries, with one hump. Camels are valuable animals in desert climates because they can carry goods and people where no vehicle can go.

How deserts form

Different kinds of deserts are formed in different ways, but always for the same reason – the air above them is too dry for it to rain. There are four main types of deserts, but once formed, the wind and any rain that may fall shape the deserts in various ways. This process is called erosion.

Changing shapes
The rounded ends of crescent dunes (1) point in the direction the wind is blowing. Strong winds mainly from one direction form transversal dunes (2) while moderate winds from one direction form longitudinal dunes (3). Star-shaped dunes (4) are formed by winds from many directions.

1.

2.

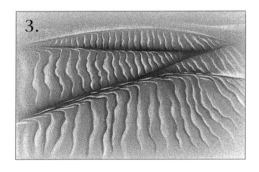
3.

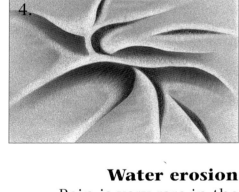
4.

Sand dunes
Desert winds can create a sandstorm. They sweep away sand and other material and dump them elsewhere. Huge mounds of sand called sand dunes are formed. They are like waves of sand.

Wind sculptures
The sand carried by the wind polishes rocks until they are round and smooth. Sometimes other incredible shapes are formed.

Water erosion
Rain is very rare in the deserts. When it does fall, it can have drastic consequences. The rain can cause sudden floods, called flash floods, in dry riverbeds. The water forms channels and arches in the rock.

Plant fixers
Bare sand dunes change shape all the time with the wind. If plants take root on the dune, they may become fixed. Then the dune no longer shifts.

Subtropical deserts

These deserts lie between 20° and 30° north and south of the equator, for example, the Sahara Desert. When the air at the equator heats up in the sun, it expands and rises. This air gets cooler as it moves away from the tropics and drops rain. By the time it reaches some subtropical areas, the air is too dry to carry any rain.

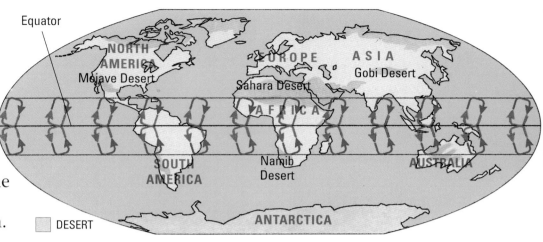

Equator

DESERT

Rainshadow deserts

A rainshadow desert, for example, the Mojave Desert in North America, forms on the leeward sides of mountain ranges. Moist winds are forced to rise by the mountains. As they rise, the air cools, clouds form, and it rains on the windward side of the range. By the time the air reaches the other side, it has lost its moisture. This dry area may form a desert The Mojave Desert lies behind the Sierra Nevada mountain range.

Dry winds

Interior deserts

There are deserts located in the middle of continents, far from the sea. By the time any winds arrive from the sea, they have already lost their water content, and no rain falls. The Gobi Desert in Asia was formed in this way.

Gobi Desert

CHINA

ARABIA

Coastal deserts

Coastal deserts can form in subtropical areas when the coast is bathed by cold ocean currents. These chill the air above them, producing a layer of fog. Although the fog and cold air are blown toward the land, the atmospheric conditions that cause rain to fall are lacking. Some coastal deserts, like the Namib Desert on the west coast of Africa, receive hardly any rain.

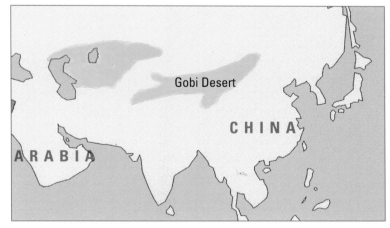

Cold air

Fog

Cold ocean current

Desert

Plant survival

Plants have adapted to desert climates in special ways so that they can survive despite low rainfall and loose soil. The green substance in plants, called chlorophyll, absorbs sunlight to help them grow. Large, flat leaves would shrivel in the desert, so some plants, like cacti, have spikes or hairs and green stems instead. Other plants, like haworthias, have deep roots designed to absorb any traces of water in the soil.

Long roots

Some desert plants, like this haworthia (above), have very long roots that can reach deep down into the soil to obtain more water.

Keeping cool

The stem of a cactus swells in order to hold as much water as possible. Its trunk is green, which means it makes its food using sunlight. The water inside the cactus supports the plant in the ground. Cacti are often covered with a thick, waxy coat of hair. This prevents them from losing too much water through evaporation (heating up and going into the air).

Creepy roots

Some cacti have many shallow roots, which spread out a long distance from the plant. This means the roots can quickly absorb the little rain that falls. They also absorb any dew that settles on the ground during the night.

Endless leaves

The strange welwitschia plant lives in scattered groups in the Namib Desert. It has only a few leathery, creeping leaves that grow up to an incredible 60 feet (18 m) long. The leaves collect dewdrops, and the plant stores the water in a giant cone-shaped root. This plant has a lifespan of one to two thousand years.

Plant thief

This plant from the Jordan Desert does not need leaves. Instead of making its own food, the broomrape, (shown left) steals food by inserting its roots into those of another plant, and drawing out the sap. The plant is a true parasite.

A little help from the birds and bees

Like all plants, cacti must be pollinated – have pollen put in their flowers – in order to make seeds. Insects adapted to desert life pollinate the plants. Birds, like this pink-headed cockatoo, eat the seeds from the cacti, fly away, and later excrete the seeds. The seeds survive, land in a new place, and grow.

When is a cactus not a cactus?

The answer is when it's a euphorbia, a typical plant from the African and Indian deserts. It looks very much like a cactus, but inside, the euphorbia holds milky sap in its thick stem, rather than water. The sap does not evaporate easily and helps the plant to hold moisture. A euphorbia usually has spines that discourage hungry animals from eating its fleshy parts.

13

Chilling out, warming up

In the summer, the temperature in tropical deserts is incredibly high during the day. In the winter, it can fall to as low as 43°F (6° C), which is quite cold. Every day there is a difference of about 36°F (20°C) between daytime and nighttime temperatures. Animals have to cope with these huge swings in temperature. They have had to come up with some pretty smart ways to protect themselves from too much heat or cold.

Dancing lizards
In the middle of the day, the sand is extremely hot to walk on. The sand-diving lizard holds two feet in the air at a time to cool itself.

A very personal parasol
The African ground squirrel holds its bushy tail over its body. It uses its tail like a parasol to protect itself from the sun's burning rays.

Big ears
Many animals that live in hot climates have big feet or ears. This American jackrabbit has large ears, with blood vessels close to the surface. Much heat is lost from the large surface of the ears. This helps to keep the animal cool.

Going for a morning run
The roadrunner is a favorite bird of the North American and Mexican deserts. This fast animal runs to catch its prey and escape – but also to help warm itself up after the cold night.

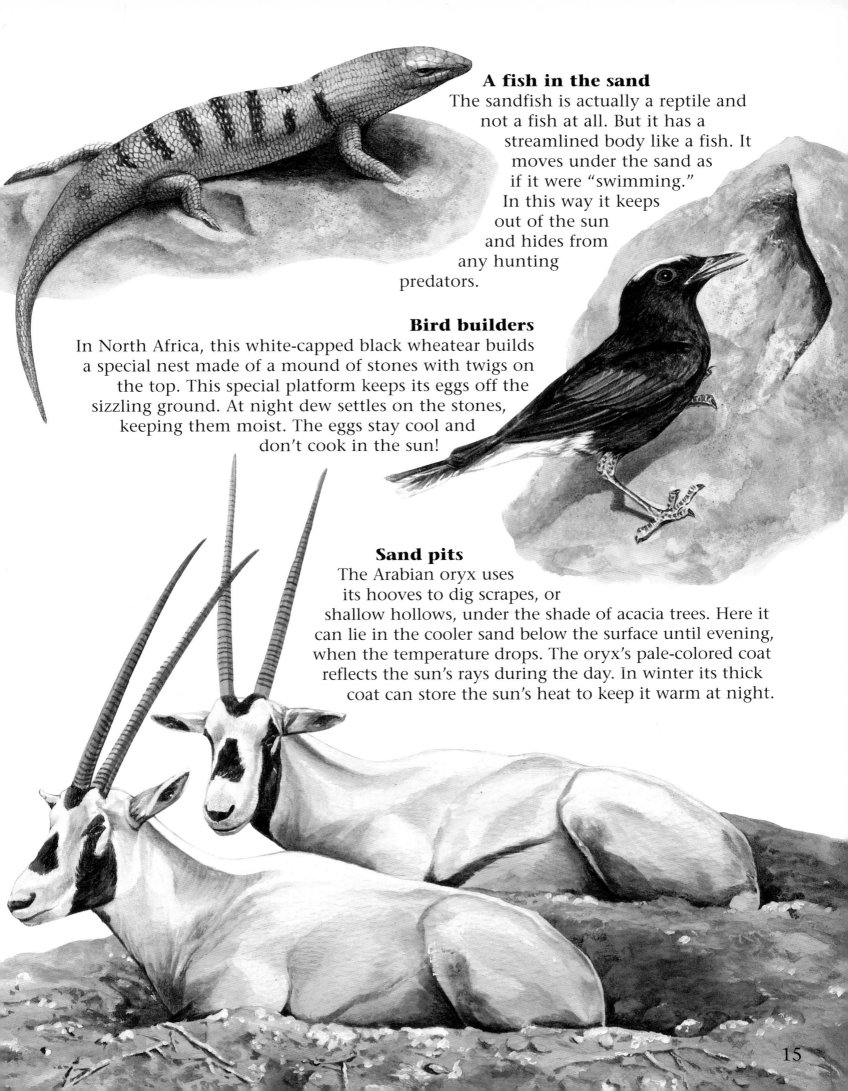

A fish in the sand

The sandfish is actually a reptile and not a fish at all. But it has a streamlined body like a fish. It moves under the sand as if it were "swimming." In this way it keeps out of the sun and hides from any hunting predators.

Bird builders

In North Africa, this white-capped black wheatear builds a special nest made of a mound of stones with twigs on the top. This special platform keeps its eggs off the sizzling ground. At night dew settles on the stones, keeping them moist. The eggs stay cool and don't cook in the sun!

Sand pits

The Arabian oryx uses its hooves to dig scrapes, or shallow hollows, under the shade of acacia trees. Here it can lie in the cooler sand below the surface until evening, when the temperature drops. The oryx's pale-colored coat reflects the sun's rays during the day. In winter its thick coat can store the sun's heat to keep it warm at night.

15

After the rain

What may seem like a dry, barren land will suddenly burst into life soon after a rainfall. Since water is essential for life, many desert plants and animals have special ways of making the most of the precious rain when it arrives. They spring into action during this short period of wet weather.

Patient toads
Spadefoot toads in the North American deserts dig a burrow using the "spades" on their back feet. The toads lie quite still there, protected by a slimy sac. They wait for up to nine months for the next rains.

Expandable cactus
This spiky cactus stores as much water as it can. It swells out until it is shaped like a barrel. As the cactus gradually uses up its private water supply, it takes on its normal, thinner shape again.

Ocean of sand
Sometimes, saltwater lakes occur in deserts. Some water animals have adapted to these very harsh conditions. When the lakes are dry, the eggs of saltwater shrimp (artemesia) can lie waiting for years. When it rains, they hatch and complete their short life cycles.

River of life
Old wadis, or riverbeds, are the perfect place for plants to survive. They can absorb any remaining water with their long roots. When the rains come, they are in the best place to get the water as soon as it arrives.

The need for speed

Some desert plants and animals have to grow and give new life as quickly as they can. Tadpole shrimp in North America lay their eggs in a pool of water. The pool dries up, but the eggs can survive for many years. When it rains again, the pool fills up. The shrimp hatch, breed, and die in just 20–40 days, before their little pool of water dries out.

It's all in the timing

Spring is the best time for birds to bring up their young because there is an ample supply of food around. But in the desert the best time is right after the rain. Zebra finches are experts in perfect timing. They breed quickly just after the rain, when the desert offers the most food for their young.

Vibrant colors

The desert bursts into bloom after the rain. One of the most spectacular sights in the Australian desert is the Sturt's Pea. The bright red flowers attract insects to pollinate them. The red color warns animals not to eat the flowers.

Hunters of the desert

There is not a lot of food to be found in the desert. Predators have to be very fast or have special weapons or skills if they are to survive.

Sting in the tail

Scorpions are well adapted to living in dry conditions. The color of their bodies blends in perfectly with the sand and stones, hiding them from their victims. Usually scorpions hunt by night. First the scorpion catches its prey with its pincers. Then it paralyzes it (stops it from moving) with the stinger in the tip of its tail. The venom of some African and Mexican scorpions is so strong that it can be fatal to human beings.

Super-sized spiders

Huge tarantula spiders roam the deserts of the Americas, and are feared for their painful bites. But if it is not hungry, the tarantula will flee rather than attack. These spiders hunt, and they bite their prey with their sharp fangs.

Little by little

Hedgehogs may not appear to be fierce predators. But hedgehogs, like desert rats, must obtain the water they need by eating lots and lots of insects.

Wide open spaces

Finding food is hard work for coyotes that live in the deserts of the Americas. In the grasslands where they also live, there is plenty of food and they need only small hunting grounds. But the desert provides little food, and the coyote must defend a much larger area if it is to find enough to eat.

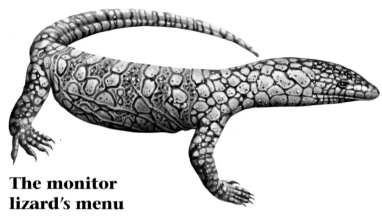

Lanner falcon

The lanner falcon of the African deserts is an impressive predator. When it sees its prey, it nosedives from a height of about 2,000 feet (600 m) to grasp the bird, lizard, or rodent, in its strong claws. The falcon can also snatch a meal from the water. If it cannot find larger prey, the falcon will feed on grasshoppers.

The monitor lizard's menu

Some lizards have adapted to living in deserts where there is only 8 inches (200 mm) of rain a year. The giant monitor lizard lives in the Australian desert. It can reach 8 feet (2.4 m) in length. This heavy, powerful lizard has strong legs for chasing its prey, and a mouth full of teeth. It will eat anything it can tear apart with its teeth and gulp down. The monitor's meals range from insects, small mammals, and birds, to other reptiles.

Rattled rattlesnake

Rattlesnakes are deaf and mostly rely on temperature as a way of finding their prey. They are able to sense the warmth of a nearby animal. Rattlesnakes rattle the tips of their tails when they sense danger, warning large animals that they are there. The snake benefits because it does not get trampled on. The rattle is made up of rings of skin, which remain behind when the snake molts (sheds its outer layer of skin). The more rings a snake has, the older it is.

Fennec

The fennec of North Africa can safely go out hunting during the day because the color of its coat reflects the sun's rays. It loses heat from its big ears to keep cool. These ears also allow it to hear the faintest sounds in the desert and find its prey. Fennecs are the tiniest of foxes and are very agile. A fennec can catch a rabbit bigger than itself.

19

Hard case

Usually we think of turtles as living near water, but even these animals have adapted to desert living. The large African spurred turtle covers its head, neck, and feet with saliva (spit) to keep cool. The desert tortoise of North America digs long burrows. The burrows lead to a huge chamber that the turtle shares with other animals, such as different reptiles, toads, rats, and insects. Turtles can pull their soft body parts into their hard shells to protect themselves from the sharp claws and beaks of predators.

Survival skills

Desert animals have to cope with a harsh environment. They manage to survive extreme heat with little water, and they can endure the chilly nights. Some also have to protect themselves from predators.

Cunning camouflage

Pebble plants have only two leaves, round and flat just like the stones of the desert. This confuses any hungry animals looking for tasty leaves to eat.

Sharp spines

The crested porcupine wards off its predators with its long spines. When the spines are raised, they make the animal look big and scary.

A prickly perch

The American turtle dove has made its home in the desert. It builds its nest at the top of a cactus so that predators cannot easily get to its young. It can cope with the heat – and also uncomfortable prickles!

Big head

The dragon-like frilled lizard of the Australian desert has large skin flaps around its neck. In the face of a dangerous predator, the lizard stretches the skin flaps out so that it looks bigger and more dangerous.

The great pretenders

The stone curlew, or thickknee, is quite at home on barren lands. It risks its life to protect its young by pretending to have a broken wing. Predators then go after the adult bird rather than the bird's eggs or babies.

High jumps

The hind legs of the kangaroo rat allow it to jump suddenly away from any predators. Although it is as small as a mouse, it can jump as far as 6.5 feet (2 m) in a single leap.

Stand up to the enemy

Although the gould monitor lizard kills prey itself, it too has enemies. When it comes face to face with a predator, it rears up on its hind legs and looks frightfully fierce. If this tactic is successful, the predator will not bother to attack.

Red for danger

Color is one way nature warns against harm. This mite's bright red body tells predators that it could be poisonous.

21

Living storage

When there is plenty of food, honeypot worker ants in the deserts of North America feed on a sugary liquid that other ants bring to the nest. The worker ants store this liquid in their huge, swollen abdomens. When food is scarce, all the members of the ant colony tap their honeypot companions with their antennae. The workers give them a drop of sugary liquid.

Food and water

Because food and water are so scarce in the desert, plants and animals have had to discover where to find them – and how to store them for the hard times ahead.

Dew collectors

Mist blowing in from the sea and the morning dew are usually the only sources of water in the desert. This ice plant from South Africa is covered with tiny pits that capture water and keep its leaves cool. The bubbles of water make the plant sparkle in the sunshine.

Surprise attack

The Australian marsupial mole digs burrows in the desert. It often feeds on the burrowing larvae of beetles. It can also sense insects above ground and jumps out suddenly to grab them.

Drastic measures

The branches of the quiver tree (above) in the Namib Desert are covered with a whitish powder, that reflects the sun's rays. In severe drought, the quiver tree loses some of its rosettes (rose-shaped groups of leaves) to stop itself from losing water. The branches that lose their rosettes can never grow new ones. But there are still enough rosettes left on the tree for it to survive until the next rain.

Swarming feeders

Desert locusts in Africa and Asia can travel long distances in huge swarms. The locusts can fly upward to around 5,000 feet (1,500 m), forming a giant tower of insects. When they land, they eat all the plants in sight.

Drinking from the air

The Darkling beetle of the Namib Desert has found the perfect way to get a drink. When the morning mist arrives, it stands head down. The dew collects on its body and runs down the grooves on its back to its mouth.

Long-distance traveler

Gundis, which are rodents, live among stony rocks in the deserts of North Africa. They do not store food, nor do they have extra fat as a reserve. They have to travel long distances in search of fresh food supplies, sometimes over half a mile (0.8 km) each morning. They feed early in the day when the plants they eat are full of moisture. Gundis rest in the heat of the day.

Special adaptations

The camel stores fat in its hump (see p.9). It has thick eyelashes to protect its eyes from sand blown by the wind, and can open and close its nostrils at will. Thick pads on its knees let the camel kneel without harming its skin, and wide hooves on its feet stop it from sinking into the sand.

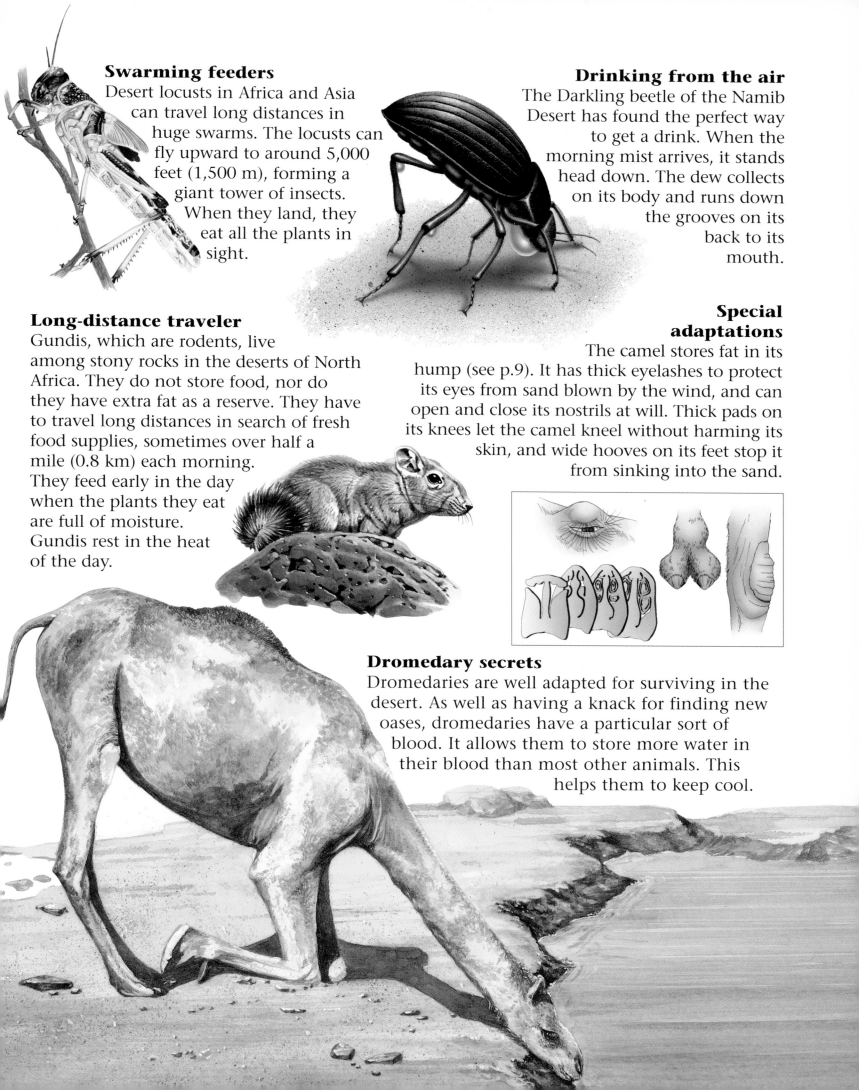

Dromedary secrets

Dromedaries are well adapted for surviving in the desert. As well as having a knack for finding new oases, dromedaries have a particular sort of blood. It allows them to store more water in their blood than most other animals. This helps them to keep cool.

The desert after dark

When the sun begins to set in the west, the burning heat gives way to more comfortable temperatures. At dusk the desert comes alive. Many animals that have avoided the heat of the day come out to feed.

Agile stalker

The lynx, or bobcat, of the American deserts is lazy by day. Its sandy-red coat makes it almost invisible against the desert. Nighttime is the perfect time to hunt. The lynx has excellent eyesight and its long ears catch the slightest sounds. It springs on its prey in a flash.

Pollination in the dark

Bats come out when evening falls. They produce sounds from their noses and listen to the returning echoes – this is called echolocation. It helps them to figure out where nearby objects and prey are located. Some desert cacti open their flowers at night. The bats pollinate the flowers with their long tongues as they lick up the insects found within.

Fit for desert life

The graceful kit fox lives in the North American deserts. At night it hunts rabbits and hares. Its long ears are typical of foxes that live in hot climates, and help to release heat from their bodies.

Small is beautiful

Deserts around the world have their own kinds of small mammals. These creatures have long hind legs that allow them to jump over the sand easily. They usually come out of their burrows at night. Desert rats live in America, gophers in the semi-deserts of Central America and Mexico, and gerbils in the deserts of Africa and Asia. If alarmed, the Mongolian gerbil beats the ground with its back legs or lets out a shrill.

Poisonous lizard

The Gila monster (or beaded lizard) of the American Mojave Desert is the only lizard that uses venom to kill its prey. For most of the day, it stays in its burrow, out of direct sunlight. The lizard comes out at night to hunt for small mammals, birds, and eggs.

What a scream!

The hairy screaming armadillo has adapted to a varied desert diet. It eats insects and small animals, and the roots and tubers (underground food stores) of plants. The armadillo will often travel long distances at night in search of dinner. Many kinds of armadillos have hair on their plates that surround their bodies. Hairy armadillos can keep warm and hold in moisture in harsh and dry environments.

Open house
To avoid the blazing sun during the day, the Saharan sand cat sleeps in hollows in the sand or in rough dens among the stones. It often shares its home with other desert animals, such as the fennec.

Insect builders
When there is mud available, female potter wasps work quickly to model their nests before the mud dries. Desert potter wasps build the same nest design as potter wasps in wetter climates.

Nests and burrows

With no trees and few bushes around, desert animals manage to make the most of what is available to them. They use nature's materials such as rocks and plants to make their homes.

Living together
Meercats in the Kalahari desert live in large family groups, sharing underground burrows. They stay in groups above ground too. Meercats rarely stray far from their homes. They take turns standing guard.

Cactus peckers

The Gila woodpecker and the gilded flicker of North America do not nest in trees. Instead, they peck out long tunnels in Saguaro cacti. The tunnels end in cool chambers lined with cactus pulp (flesh). When the woodpeckers leave, other animals, such as the pygmy owl and ash-throated flycatcher, are quick to move in.

A ready-made home

Even woodrats have adapted to desert life. The desert woodrat lives in cracks and crevices it finds in the rocks. It can also build its nest in a cactus, using pieces of the plant itself. Predators are unlikely to risk the prickles to attack the nest.

Anywhere will do

The budgerigars of Australia rarely stay in the same place for long. Sometimes they venture into deserts. These birds make nests in holes in plants, without even lining them for comfort.

Hidden danger

The antlion looks rather like a beautiful butterfly as an adult. Yet, as a larva, it is an extremely ferocious beast. It digs a steep funnel-shaped pit in the sand. When ants and other insects walk over the edge, they tumble down into the trap. The antlion quickly seizes them and gobbles them up.

Navigating ants

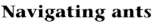

The desert ants of the Sahara live in cool underground burrows. They must surface during the day to find something to eat. When they look for food they zigzag across the sand, but they always manage to find the shortest way home. The ants have learned to use the sun's rays to figure out where they are. They stop and turn their heads from side to side to check the light from the sun. Without this skill, the ants would soon get lost and burn up.

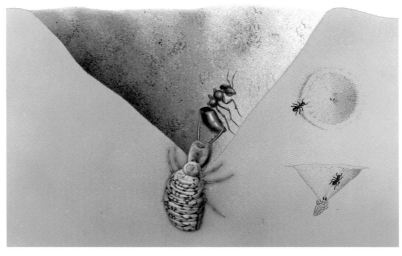

Desert babies

Life is hard in the desert. In such difficult conditions, parents usually take special care of their babies to make sure that they survive.

Helpless

Many rodents, such as the deer mouse, are born blind and helpless. The deer mouse lives in dry areas of the Americas. A female deer mouse can have four litters of four to six young every year. She must eat a lot of food (seeds, berries, and insects). The father also helps to raise the babies.

Growing dark with age

The female camel is pregnant for 12 to 14 months and has just one baby. She feeds it with her milk for a year. Camels reach adulthood when they are 10 to 12 years old. Baby camels are a pale beige color when they are born. Their coats darken as they grow older.

Free ride

A mother scorpion carries her young huddled together on her back. The babies can absorb water from her skin. This stops them from drying out in the heat.

The Indian onager

Asian wild donkeys, called Indian onagers, feed on plants and grasses of the Indian deserts. A mother onager is pregnant for 11 to 12 months, and has just one foal. Like many other young hoofed animals, the onager learns to stand and run very soon after it is born. It lives close to its mother for one or two years.

Fluffy feathers

This owlet is a baby elf owl. It has a good view over the Saguaro desert region of Arizona. The baby's nest is in an old woodpecker's hole in a cactus. As an owlet it has white feathers, but the feathers gradually change to brown as it grows up.

Hatching from an egg

Birds are not the only babies to hatch from eggs. Most snakes, such as true and false coral snakes from the deserts in North America, hatch from eggs too. Reptile eggs have leathery shells instead of hard ones like bird eggs.

Sharing childcare

The sandgrouse lives mostly in Africa and the Middle East. The female usually cares for the young in the nest. The male flies 12 to 20 miles (20 to 30 km) from the nest to collect water. He absorbs it using specially adapted feathers on his chest. When he returns, his fledglings run to him for a drink of water.

Wild dogs

Dingos are tawny-reddish wild dogs that live in different habitats in Australia. Some have moved into the desert. Dingos give birth to a litter of five to nine pups in a den. The pups drink their mother's milk for two months. They stay with their parents for at least a year, joining in the hunt for food.

29

At the oasis

An oasis is an area of fresh water in the middle of a desert. Some oases are just tiny springs with a few palm trees around them. Others are so big that they can be used to irrigate land and supply water for towns. Offering water and shade, oases are important stopover points in the desert for both people and animals.

Tongue trap

The Namaqua chameleon lives in the Namib Desert of southern Africa. When insects and small animals come to the oasis, the chameleon traps them with its long tongue.

Amazing fish

Some fish can even live in the desert. Walking catfish (in Africa and Asia) can wiggle from one puddle of water to another. First they lift the front of their bodies with their fins. Then they push themselves along the ground with their tails. While they're out of the water, they can breathe air through their skin.

How an oasis forms

The water at oases comes from underground sources that build up above layers of impermeable rock. The water seeps up through cracks or faults in the rock.

underground water

fault

Shady palms

Date palms are grown in African deserts for their fruit. They can grow to 66 feet (20 m) in height and live as long as 200 years. Palm trees offer welcome shade as well as fruit.

Desert vulture

The small Egyptian vulture sometimes flies to an oasis from nearby semidesert areas. When one bird finds a dead or dying animal it swoops down for its meal. Others that notice the vulture swooping down will follow to grab a share of the meal.

A safe place to nest

Emerald toads live in oases where the water never dries up completely. There they can safely lay their eggs. During the day they hide under stones, coming out only at night to catch insects for food.

The traveling addax

The addax is a large antelope with a grayish coat in summer and a darker coat in winter. It has twisted, backward-slanting horns. Broad hooves help it walk over sand. The rare addax lives in sandy and stony parts of the Sahara Desert. These animals have a wonderful ability to find patches of plant life. They will travel miles to reach an oasis that has plants to feed on.

31

Delicate deserts

Deserts are harsh, barren places. They produce little food, and the conditions there are difficult. But deserts have their own wildlife that has taken millions of years to evolve. The wildlife is well adapted to life in this habitat. The desert ecosystem – a community of plants and animals – is finely balanced. We must be careful to keep it this way, otherwise desert species may become extinct.

Plant thieves

Cactus collecting is a popular hobby. Some people dig up rare species in the wild, such as the beautiful silver dollar cactus (above). If too many are removed, there may be no more plants in the future.

Spreading sands

People in dry areas near deserts may destroy plants and trees to create farmland, which uses up water. When this happens, the desert may spread to this new area.

Oil in the desert

Valuable oil lies under the sands of many deserts. Using the profits from selling oil, some countries can irrigate (bring water to) the deserts by pumping water out from underground. This happens in the Sahara Desert in Libya. But the water will not be renewed, and will last for only about 50 years.

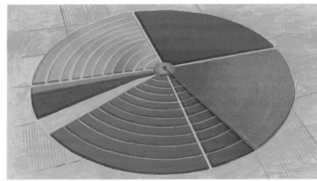

Circular spray irrigation

Farmers in the desert have a desperate need for water to irrigate their crops. A water supply, called a water table, found deep below the earth's surface and formed millions of years ago, is used for a process called circular spray irrigation (shown above). Once this water supply is used up it cannot be replenished, and the desert will become even drier.

Newcomers take over

The prickly pear cactus originally came from the Americas. It was taken to Australia as an ornamental plant and for building natural fences. With no natural enemies to eat it, the plant grew so successfully that it soon spread everywhere. To control it, cactus moths were introduced. The larvae ate the cacti, and cacti numbers began to fall. Before bringing a new plant or animal into a country, it is important to think about what could happen.

At risk

The African wild donkey (shown above) is a shy animal that lives in the Horn of Africa. Although they are already a protected species, the donkeys are still in danger. The local inhabitants hunt them for their meat and skin.

Success story

Animals in danger of extinction can be helped. In 1972 there were no Arabian oryxes left in the Arabian Desert. They were bred in captivity and returned to their habitat.

Desert locusts

Locusts sometimes form a massive group of millions of animals, called a swarm. They fly around together, eating all the desert plants they find. When this happens, trees and shrubs are left bare. Other animals have a hard time surviving after the locusts have eaten all the plants.

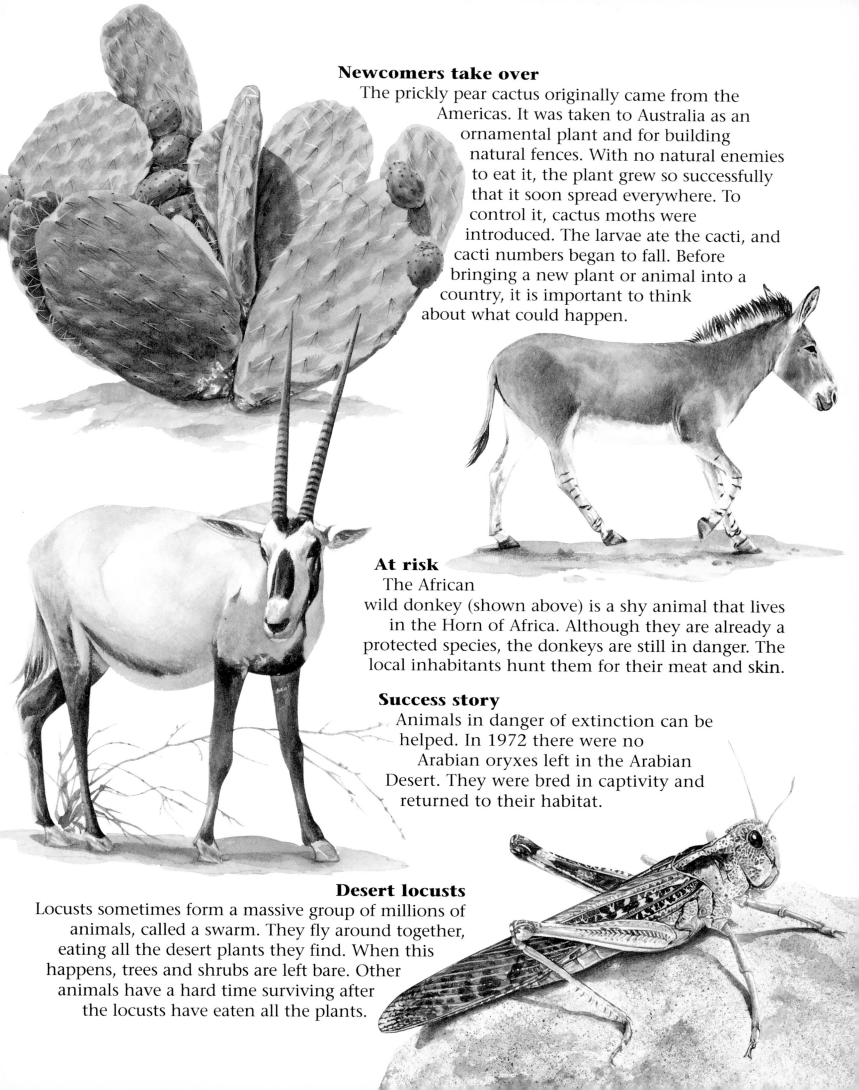

THE DESERT GAME

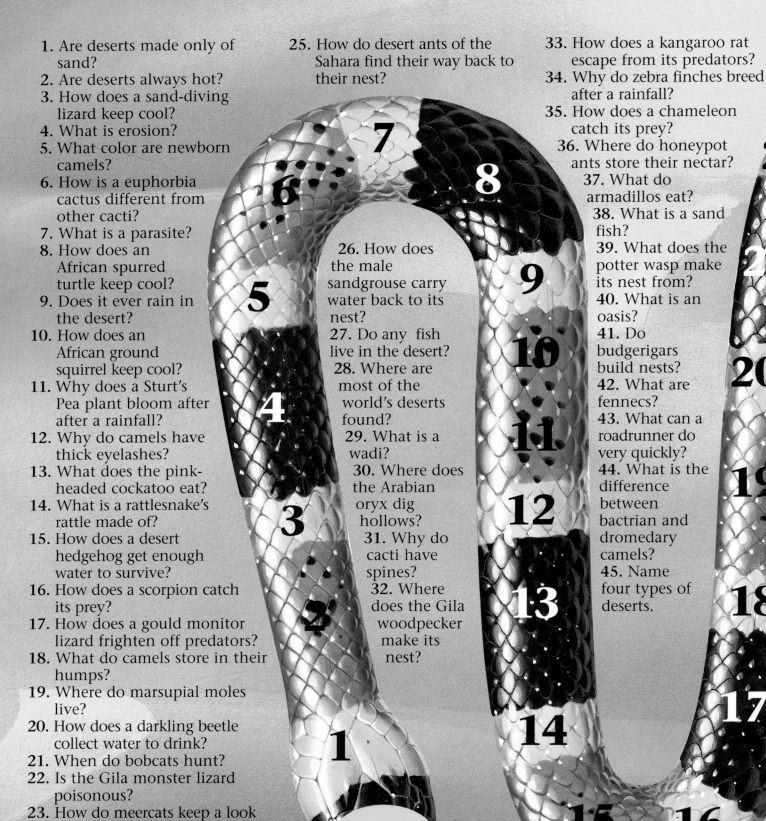

1. Are deserts made only of sand?
2. Are deserts always hot?
3. How does a sand-diving lizard keep cool?
4. What is erosion?
5. What color are newborn camels?
6. How is a euphorbia cactus different from other cacti?
7. What is a parasite?
8. How does an African spurred turtle keep cool?
9. Does it ever rain in the desert?
10. How does an African ground squirrel keep cool?
11. Why does a Sturt's Pea plant bloom after after a rainfall?
12. Why do camels have thick eyelashes?
13. What does the pink-headed cockatoo eat?
14. What is a rattlesnake's rattle made of?
15. How does a desert hedgehog get enough water to survive?
16. How does a scorpion catch its prey?
17. How does a gould monitor lizard frighten off predators?
18. What do camels store in their humps?
19. Where do marsupial moles live?
20. How does a darkling beetle collect water to drink?
21. When do bobcats hunt?
22. Is the Gila monster lizard poisonous?
23. How do meercats keep a look out for danger?
24. What is a dingo?

25. How do desert ants of the Sahara find their way back to their nest?
26. How does the male sandgrouse carry water back to its nest?
27. Do any fish live in the desert?
28. Where are most of the world's deserts found?
29. What is a wadi?
30. Where does the Arabian oryx dig hollows?
31. Why do cacti have spines?
32. Where does the Gila woodpecker make its nest?

33. How does a kangaroo rat escape from its predators?
34. Why do zebra finches breed after a rainfall?
35. How does a chameleon catch its prey?
36. Where do honeypot ants store their nectar?
37. What do armadillos eat?
38. What is a sand fish?
39. What does the potter wasp make its nest from?
40. What is an oasis?
41. Do budgerigars build nests?
42. What are fennecs?
43. What can a roadrunner do very quickly?
44. What is the difference between bactrian and dromedary camels?
45. Name four types of deserts.

This game can be played by one player, or by two or more people taking turns. You will need a die to roll, and playing pieces (for example, pennies, small stones, or colorful beads.) Each person should choose a playing piece to begin.

You are lost in the desert! The object of the game is to reach the oasis before any other player by following the path along the snake's body. Begin at the snake's head marked START. Throw the die and move foward along the path the same number of spaces that the die shows. Answer the question correctly and you may take another turn. If you answer incorrectly, stay where you landed and allow the next person a turn.

Continue in this manner until a player reaches the end of the trail and the last question. In order for you to move foward to the snake's tail and enter the oasis, you must answer the last question correctly.

23

24

25

26

27

28

29

30

31

32

33

34

35

36

37

38

39

40

41

42

43

44

45

FINISH

**WELL DONE!
YOU HAVE
MADE IT TO
THE OASIS**

Answers to the game

1. No. Deserts have boulders and rocks as well.

2. No. Desert temperatures can drop to the freezing point at night.

3. The sand-diving lizard holds two feet in the air at a time to cool itself.

4. Erosion is the wearing away of rock or sand by wind or rain.

5. Camels are a pale beige color at birth.

6. A euphorbia cactus stores a milky sap in its stem instead of water.

7. A parasite is a plant or animal that lives in or on others and gets its food from them.

8. The African spurred turtle covers itself with saliva to keep cool.

9. Yes. But no more than 10 inches (25 cm) a year.

10. The African ground squirrel uses its bushy tail like a parasol.

11. The Sturt's Pea plant bursts into flower after it rains to attract insects for pollination.

12. Camels have thick eyelashes to protect their eyes from sand blown by the wind.

13. The pink-headed cockatoo eats cactus seeds.

14. The rattlesnake's rattle is made up of rings of skin left behing from molting.

15. Desert hedgehogs eat lots of insects to obtain the water they need to survive.

16. The scorpion catches its prey with its pincers then paralyzes the prey with its stinger.

17. A gould monitor lizard rears up on its hind legs to frighten off predators.

18. Camels store fat in their humps.

19. Marsupial moles live in burrows.

20. The darkling beetle collects dew on its body that runs down grooves on its back into its mouth.

21. Bobcats hunt at night.

22. Yes. The Gila monster lizard is poisonous.

23. Meercats take turns standing guard.

24. A dingo is a tawny-reddish wild dog from Australia.

25. The Saharan Desert ant uses the sun to guide it back to its nest.

26. The male sandgrouse carries water in its chest feathers.

27. Yes. The catfish lives in the desert.

28. Most deserts are found near the equator.

29. A wadi is a riverbed that is dry most of the time.

30. The oryx dig hollows under acacia trees so that they can lie in the shade.

31. Cacti have spines to stop animals from eating them.

32. The Gila woodpecker makes its nest inside the stems of cacti.

33. Kangaroo rats use their hind legs to jump suddenly away from predators.

34. Zebra finches breed just after a rainfall because that is the time when there is the most food for their young.

35. The chameleon traps its prey with its long sticky tongue.

36. Honeypot ants store nectar in their abdomens.

37. Armadillos eats insects, small animals, and the roots and tubers of plants.

38. A sand fish is actually a reptile.

39. The potter wasp makes its nest from mud.

40. An oasis is an area of fresh water in the middle of a desert.

41. No. Budgerigars make nests in holes in plants.

42. Fennecs are tiny foxes.

43. A roadrunner can run very quickly.

44. A bactrian camel has two humps; a dromedary camel has one hump.

45. The four types of deserts are 1.) subtropical; 2.) rainshadow; 3.) interior; and 4.) coastal.

Glossary

camouflage: the colors and patterns on something that match or blend in with its surroundings.

chlorophyll: the green substance in plants which helps them to make food.

dew: tiny droplets of water that form on cool surfaces between the evening and morning.

diurnal animals: animals that are active by day and sleep at night, such as the lion.

dunes: mounds or ridges of loose sand formed by the wind.

ecosystem: a place where animals and plants live and interact with their environment and with each other.

equator: an imaginary line that runs round the center of the earth.

erosion: the wearing away of rock. This can be caused by wind or water.

evaporation: the process of losing moisture into the air, often by heat.

extinction: when all the plants or animals of one species die out.

habitats: the place where a plant or animal naturally lives and grows.

inhabit: to live.

invertebrates: animals without backbones.

irrigate: supply with water.

larva: the name given to an insect after it has hatched out of an egg, but before it has reached its final stage of development. Larvae is the plural for larva.

mammals: animals that give birth to their young and raise them on the mother's milk, like mice. Mammals are usually covered in fur or hair.

marsupials: animals whose females carry around their young in a pouch, like kangaroos.

nocturnal animals: creatures that are active by night and sleep in the day, like the bat.

oasis: an area of fresh water in the middle of a desert.

parasites: plants or animals that live in or on others and feed off them.

photosynthesis: the process in which green plants use the energy from sunlight to make their food.

polar regions: areas in or near the North or South Poles.

predator: animals, like the crocodile, that kill other animals for food.

prey: animals that are hunted and eaten by other animals.

reptiles: cold-blooded animals with a hard, scaly skin, like a snake or a crocodile, that usually lay eggs.

rodents: mammals with strong front teeth for cutting, like mice.

sap: the liquid inside a plant that keeps it alive.

species: groups of plants or animals that have the same features and that can reproduce within their groups.

subtropical areas: regions bordering the tropics.

tropics: the region between the Tropic of Cancer (north of the equator) and the Tropic of Capricorn (south of the equator).

venom: poison used by some animals to kill or stun their prey.

water vapor: moisture contained in the air.

wadis: riverbeds that are dry most of the time.

Index